Spotlight on™ Articulation – CH

by Barb Truman, Lauri Whiskeyman, and Margaret Warner

Skills	Ages
■ articulation	■ 5 through 10
	Grades
	■ K through 5

Evidence-Based Practice

According to the *Clinical Guidelines of the Royal College of Speech & Language Therapists* (www.rcslt.org/resources, 2005) and the *Preferred Practice Patterns of The American Speech-Language-Hearing Association* (www.asha.org/members/deskref-journals/deskref/default, 2004):

- Acquiring effective spoken language involves the development of a range of processing skills, which utilizes multisensory information and the development of phonology and articulation.

- Speech sound intervention should focus on improvement of speech sound discrimination and production.

- Speech sound intervention should include general facilitation of newly-acquired articulation and/or phonological abilities to a variety of speaking, listening, and literacy-learning contexts.

The activities in this book incorporate the above principles and are also based on expert professional practice.

LinguiSystems®

LinguiSystems, Inc.
3100 4th Avenue
East Moline, IL 61244
800-776-4332

FAX: 800-577-4555
E-mail: service@linguisystems.com
Web: linguisystems.com

Copyright © 2006 LinguiSystems, Inc.

All of our products are copyrighted to protect the fine work of our authors. You may only copy the materials as needed for your own use with students. Any other reproduction or distribution of the pages in this book is prohibited, including copying the entire book to use as another primary source or "master" copy.

Printed in the U.S.A.

ISBN 10: 0-7606-0694-3
ISBN 13: 978-0-7606-0694-0

Table of Contents

Introduction 3

Syllable Practice
CH Syllables 4

Initial
Listen Up! (pictures) 5
CH vs. SH Pictures 6
Chalk Talk (pictures) 7
Charlie Cheetah (maze) 8
Chip, Chip, Hooray! (game) 9
CH Tic-Tac-Toe 10
Picnic Fun (rebus story) 11
Miss Childers' Class (picture scene) 12
What's Cooking? (sequence story) 13
CH Fill-In Sentences 14

Final
At the End (pictures) 15
Just Peachy (pictures) 16
Drawing Is Fun (pictures) 17
Ostrich Ranch (maze) 18
Match Around (game) 19
CH and SH Pairs 20
CH Tic-Tac-Toe 21
Wrestling Match (rebus story) 22
Back Porch (picture scene) 23
Mr. Hatch and Patch (sequence story) 24
CH Fill-In Sentences 25

Medial
CH Monster (pictures) 26
What's Your Fortune? (pictures) 27
CH, CH, CH! (game) 28
CH Tic-Tac-Toe 29
CH–ing! 30
At the Zoo (rebus story) 31
A Day at the Park (picture scene) 32
Not So Lucky Key Chain (sequence story) 33
CH Fill-In Sentences 34

Initial, Final, and Medial
CH Rows 35
Richie Helps His Dad (rebus story) 36
Go, Team, Go! (picture scene) 37
Inchy's Adventure (sequence story) 38
CH Fill-In Sentences 39

Progress Chart 40

About the Authors

Barb Truman, **Lauri Whiskeyman**, and **Margaret Warner** have collaborated together on many LinguiSystems products over the past 15 years. Barb and Lauri are speech-language pathologists who worked with children in preschool through high school before joining the LinguiSystems family. Margaret is a freelance artist and has illustrated many LinguiSystems materials.

Illustrations by Margaret Warner
Cover design by Jason Platt
Page layout by Christine Buysse

Introduction

You can never have too many materials—especially for articulation practice! It takes a lot of practice to change a student's articulation patterns. The goal of the *Spotlight on Articulation* series is to provide lots of fun practice across many levels (e.g., syllable, word, sentence).

In *Spotlight on Articulation – CH*, you'll find worksheets with pictures, words, and sentences and engaging activities (e.g., mazes, tic-tac-toes, games, rebus stories, fill-ins). We have used a variety of words to allow for practice in many different phonetic contexts. To give students more practice per word, have them repeat the word a specific number of times or do the activity page a second time.

The activity sheets are designed to be pick-up-and-use ready. They are arranged in a hierarchy by word position, but you can start wherever you wish and pick and choose the pages that suit your student's level of performance. There is a progress chart on page 40 to help you track your student's progress.

The syllable activity sheet on page 4 is versatile enough to work on the target phoneme in all positions. Have the student repeat the syllable as she touches the CH and then the vowel (e.g., "cha"). For final position practice, have the student touch the vowel and then touch the CH (e.g., "ach"). For medial practice, have the student touch the vowel, touch the CH, and then touch the vowel while phonating (e.g., "acha"). The vowels can represent long or short vowel sounds as needed for practice.

Tips for Production*

The /ch/ sound is voiceless and is produced by saying /t/, then /sh/ in rapid succession. To correctly produce this sound, the tongue must first form a bowl and raise up to the palate. The tip of the tongue and front of the tongue should touch the alveolar ridge as the sides of the tongue touch the inside of the upper teeth. In this position, the airstream is completely stopped (i.e., /t/ sound). Then the midline of the tongue is quickly lowered to create a shallow groove in the tongue. An unvoiced breath stream is released through the groove to create the /ch/ sound.

- To help the child discriminate /ch/, have her listen to minimal pairs, ideally pairs that reflect the child's error pattern (e.g., *s/sh, sh/ch, t/ch*). You can also have the child discriminate between correct and incorrect production of /ch/.

- To shape /ch/ from /sh/, have the child say /t/ then /sh/ slowly at first, then rapidly until the sounds blend together. You can also have the child try to say /t/ and /sh/ at the same time.

- If a child is lateralizing /ch/ (i.e., sounds slushy), she is directing the breath stream to the sides of the tongue and mouth rather than down the middle. The child will benefit from oral-motor exercises such as jaw stabilization and tongue exercises that involve raising the sides of the tongue and lowering the center (i.e., tongue bowl).

We hope your students enjoy these activity sheets as they practice their /ch/ sound.

Barb, Lauri, and Margaret

*adapted with permission from Plass, B. (1996). *SPARC Artic Jr.* East Moline, IL: LinguiSystems, Inc.

CH Syllables

Name _____

Touch each banana as you say CH syllables.

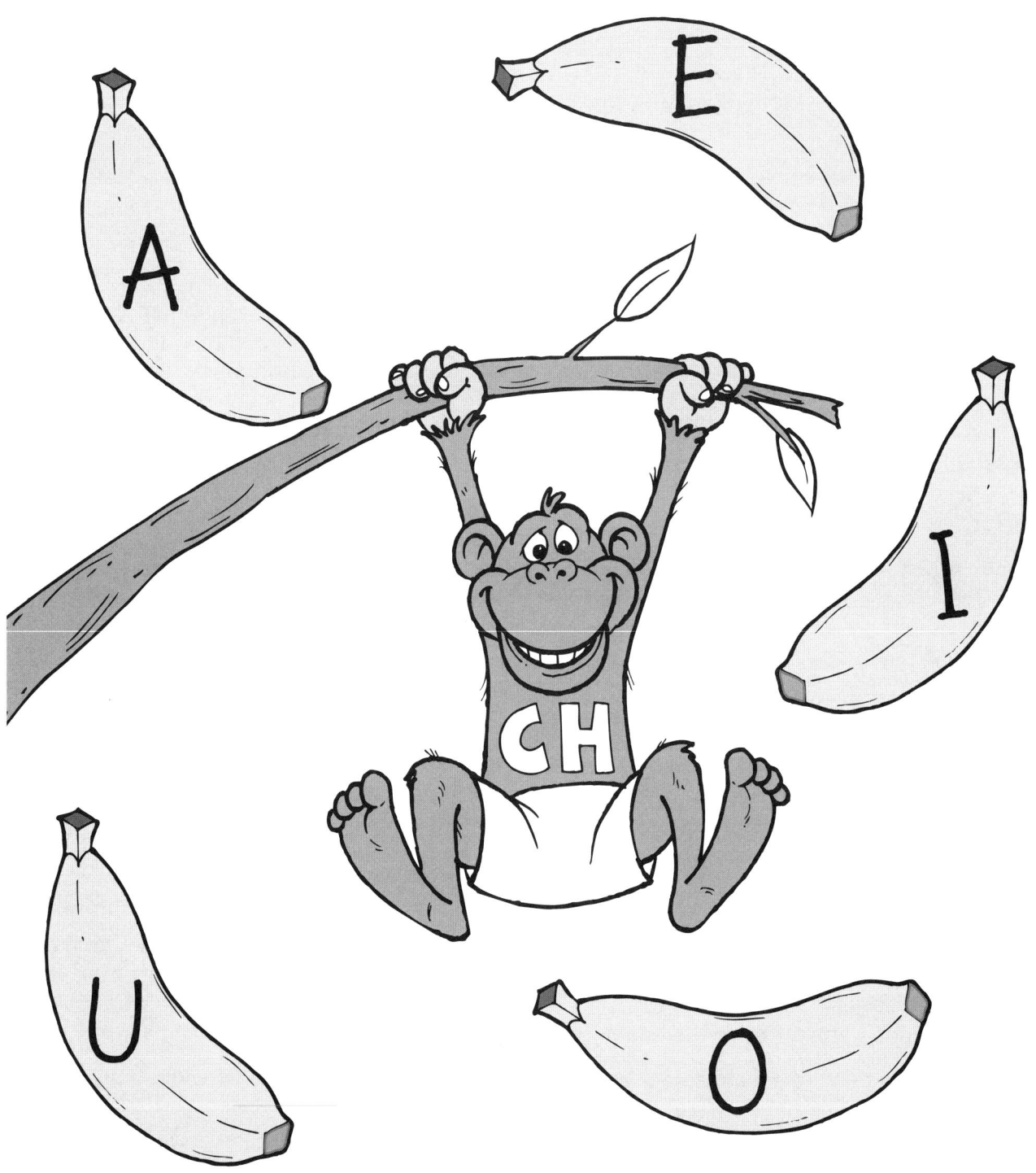

Listen Up!

Name _____

Draw a line from the CH to pictures of words beginning with the CH sound. Then name those pictures using a good CH sound.

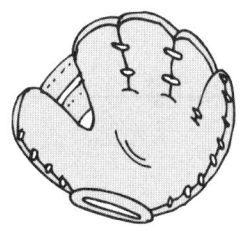
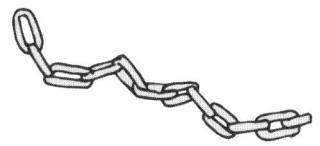

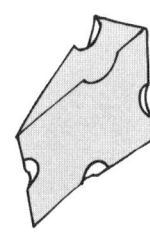

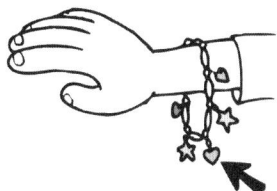

Answers: chain, chair, chalk, charm, cheek, cheese

Initial
Spotlight on Articulation – CH   5   Copyright © 2006 LinguiSystems, Inc.

CH vs. SH Pictures

Name _____

Look at the pictures in each box. Circle the picture of the word that begins with the CH sound. Then name that picture using a good CH sound.

Answers: chew, chair, cheat, chin, chip

Initial
Spotlight on Articulation – CH

Chalk Talk

Name _____

Cross out the pictures of words that don't begin with the CH sound. Then name the other pictures using a good CH sound.

Cross Out: apple, ladder, pitcher
Name: cello, cherry, chicken, chimney, chipmunk

Initial
Spotlight on Articulation – CH

Charlie Cheetah

Name _____

Show Charlie Cheetah the way home. Name as many CH pictures as you can along the way.

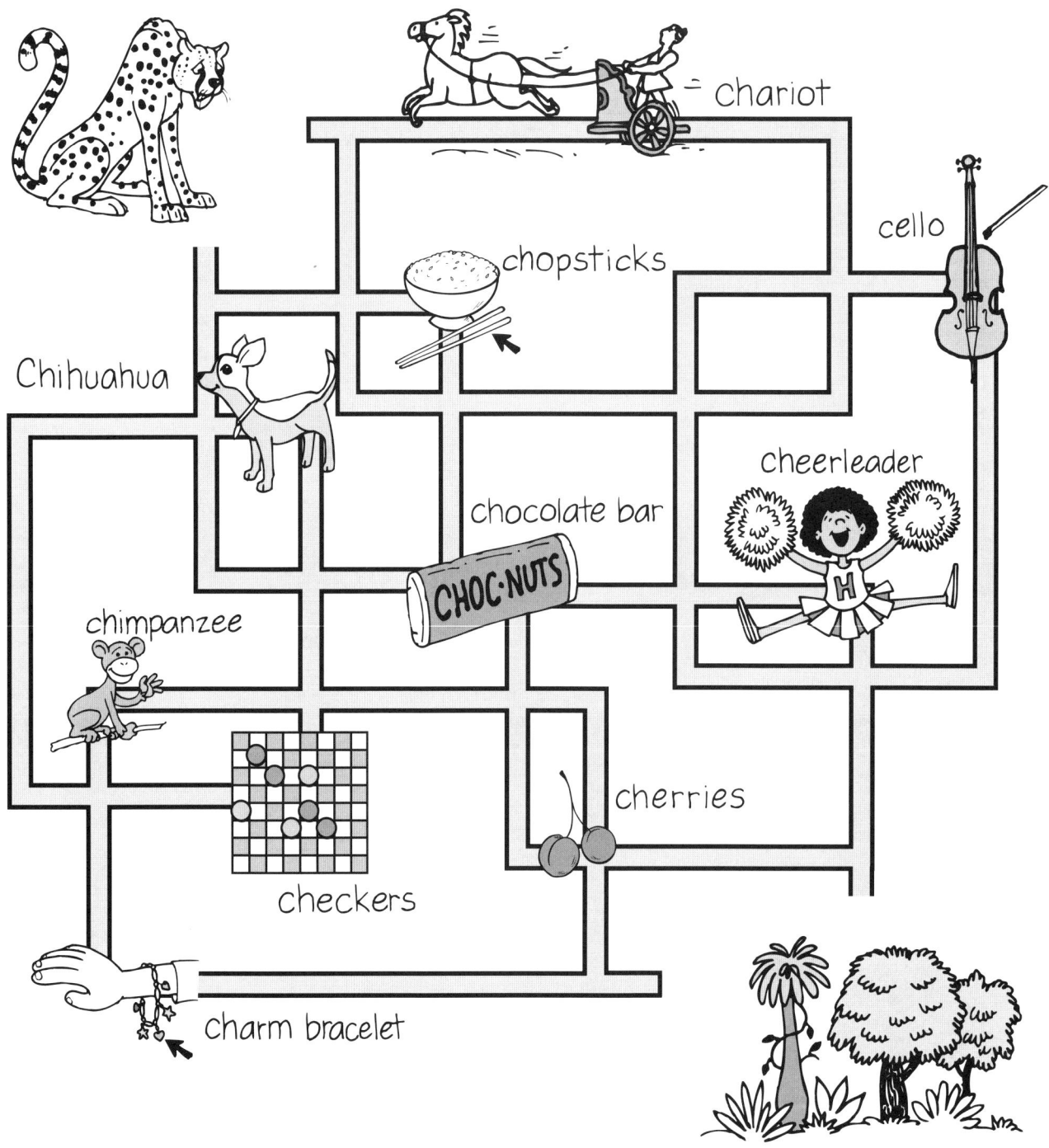

Initial
Spotlight on Articulation – CH

Copyright © 2006 LinguiSystems, Inc.

Chip, Chip, Hooray!

Name _____

Toss a penny. Heads—move one space. Tails—move two spaces. Name each picture along the way using a good CH sound.

Initial
Spotlight on Articulation – CH

CH Tic-Tac-Toe

Name _____

Listen as someone says each CH word. Find the word and say it. Then circle the CH at the beginning of the word. When you're finished, play tic-tac-toe!

chick	chips	chart
cheek	chin	chew
chalk	chain	chest

change	chair	chores
choose	chop	chunk
chant	child	chimp

chow	chilly	cheat
churn	check	chief
cheer	chase	charm

chapter	China	cherry
cheetah	chili	chopping
chariot	chisel	chicken

Initial
Spotlight on Articulation – CH

Picnic Fun

Name _____

Read this story aloud. Don't forget to use a good CH sound.

 and  went to a picnic. First they ate some . Next they
Charles   Chip   chicken

ate some . Then they ate some .
          chips   cherries

After the boys ate, they played . In the middle of their game, they
                                 chess

heard a . They saw a  in a tree. and
         chirp   chickadee   Charles   Chip   chased

the . When the  flew away, and  finished their
     chickadee   chickadee   Charles   Chip

 game.
  chess

Initial
Spotlight on Articulation – CH

Miss Childers' Class

Name _____

Find all the pictures of words that begin with the CH sound. Then tell about the picture using a good CH sound.

Key words: cello, chair, chalk, chalkboard, charm bracelet, chart, checkers, cheetah, chest, children, chimpanzee, Chip

Initial
Spotlight on Articulation – CH

What's Cooking?

Name _____

Listen to the story. Then cut the pictures apart. Put the pictures in order and retell the story. Don't forget to use a good CH sound.

Chita and Charlie were cheery as they cooked. First they made chili and cheeseburgers.

Next they made chicken with chestnuts.

Then Chita made a cherry pie and Charlie made a chocolate cake.

As Chita and Charlie ate, they talked about tomorrow's menu—clam chowder, chicken chow mein, and cheesecake!

CH Fill-In Sentences

Name _____

Say the words in the box. Fill in each sentence with a word from the box. Then say each sentence using a good CH sound.

championship	chased	chicken pox	choke
chapters	Cheating	children	chopsticks
chariots	checkup	China	chowder

1. Chance had to stay home from school because he had the _____.

2. All of the _____ were playing on the playground.

3. There were nine _____ in the book.

4. Mr. Chan went to the doctor for a _____.

5. We ate the Chinese food with _____.

6. The cat _____ the mouse around the room.

7. The football team won the state _____.

8. If you eat too fast, you could _____ on your food.

9. _____ on a test can get you kicked out of school.

10. The Romans traveled in _____.

11. The clam _____ at this restaurant is delicious.

12. Someday I hope to visit _____.

Answers: chicken pox, children, chapters, checkup, chopsticks, chased, championship, choke, Cheating, chariots, chowder, China

Initial
Spotlight on Articulation – CH

At the End

Name _____

Draw a line from the CH to pictures of words that end with the CH sound. Then name those pictures using a good CH sound.

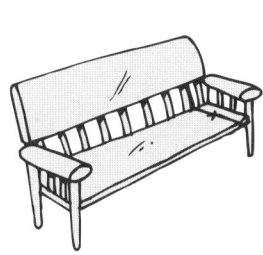
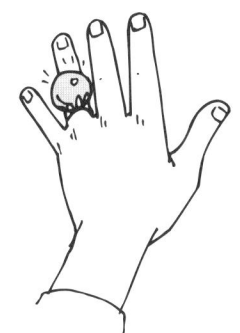

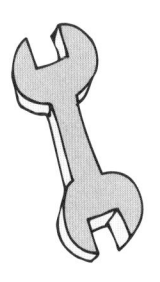

Answers: bench, branch, punch, watch, wrench

Just Peachy

Name _____

Trace the peaches with pictures of words that end with the CH sound. Then name those pictures using a good CH sound.

Answers: beach, catch, hutch, March, match, switch

Final
Spotlight on Articulation – CH

Drawing Is Fun

Name _____

Cross out the pictures of words that don't end with the CH sound. Then name the other pictures using a good CH sound.

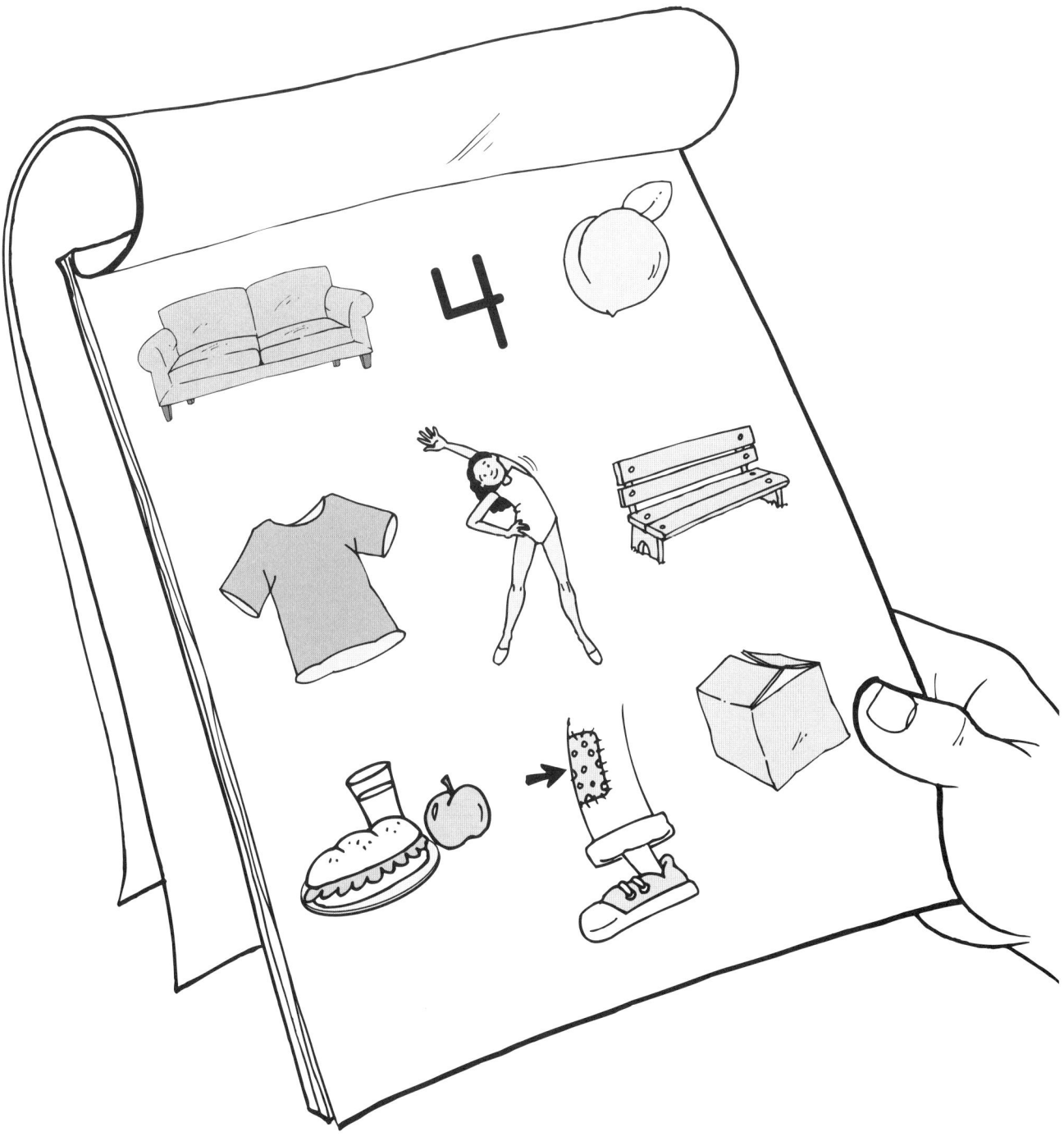

Cross Out: box, four, shirt
Name: bench, couch, lunch, patch, peach, stretch

Ostrich Ranch

Name _____

Help the cowboy get back to the ostrich ranch. Name as many CH pictures as you can along the way.

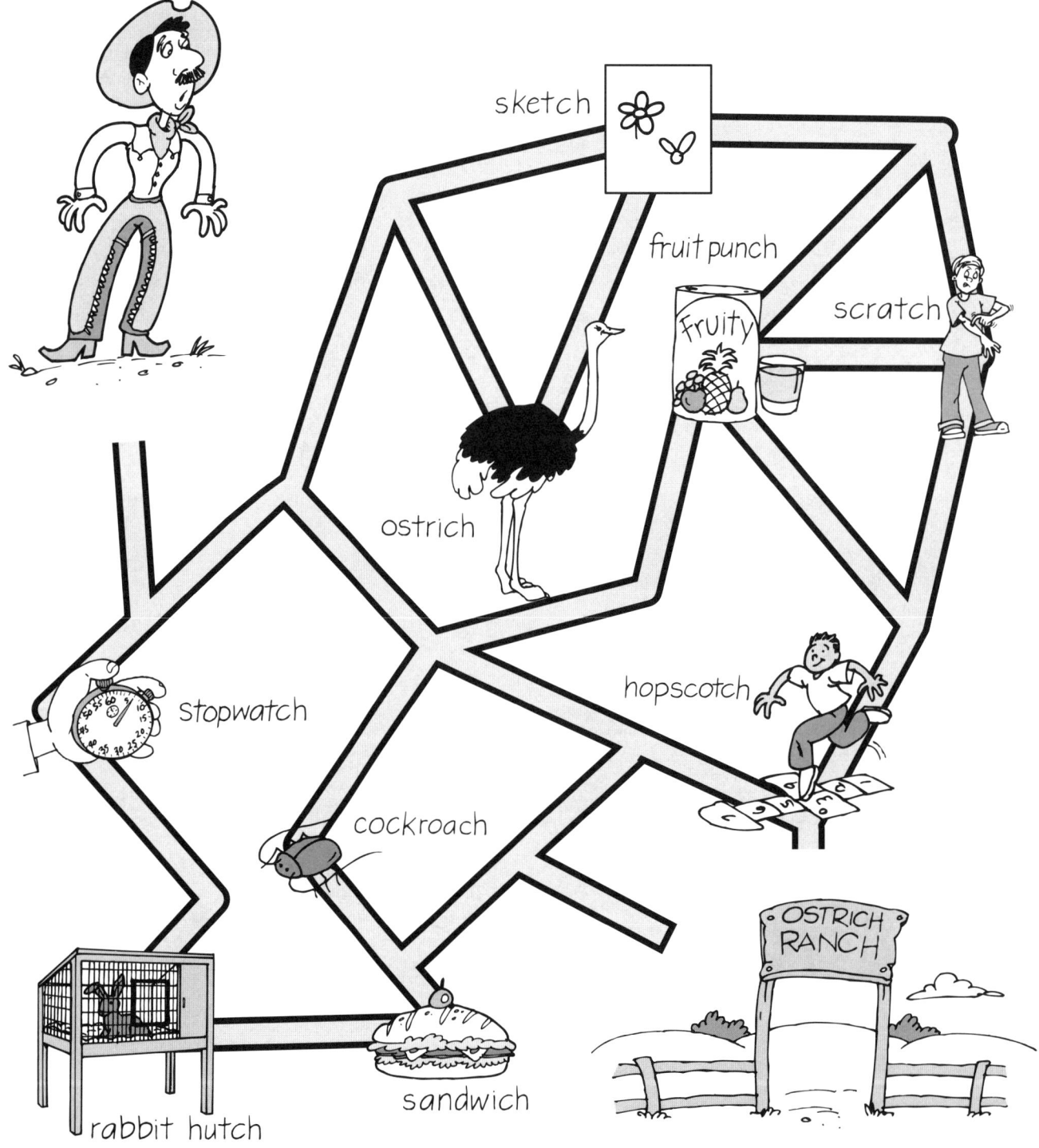

Match Around

Name _____

Toss a penny. Heads—move one space. Tails—move two spaces. Name each picture along the way using a good CH sound.

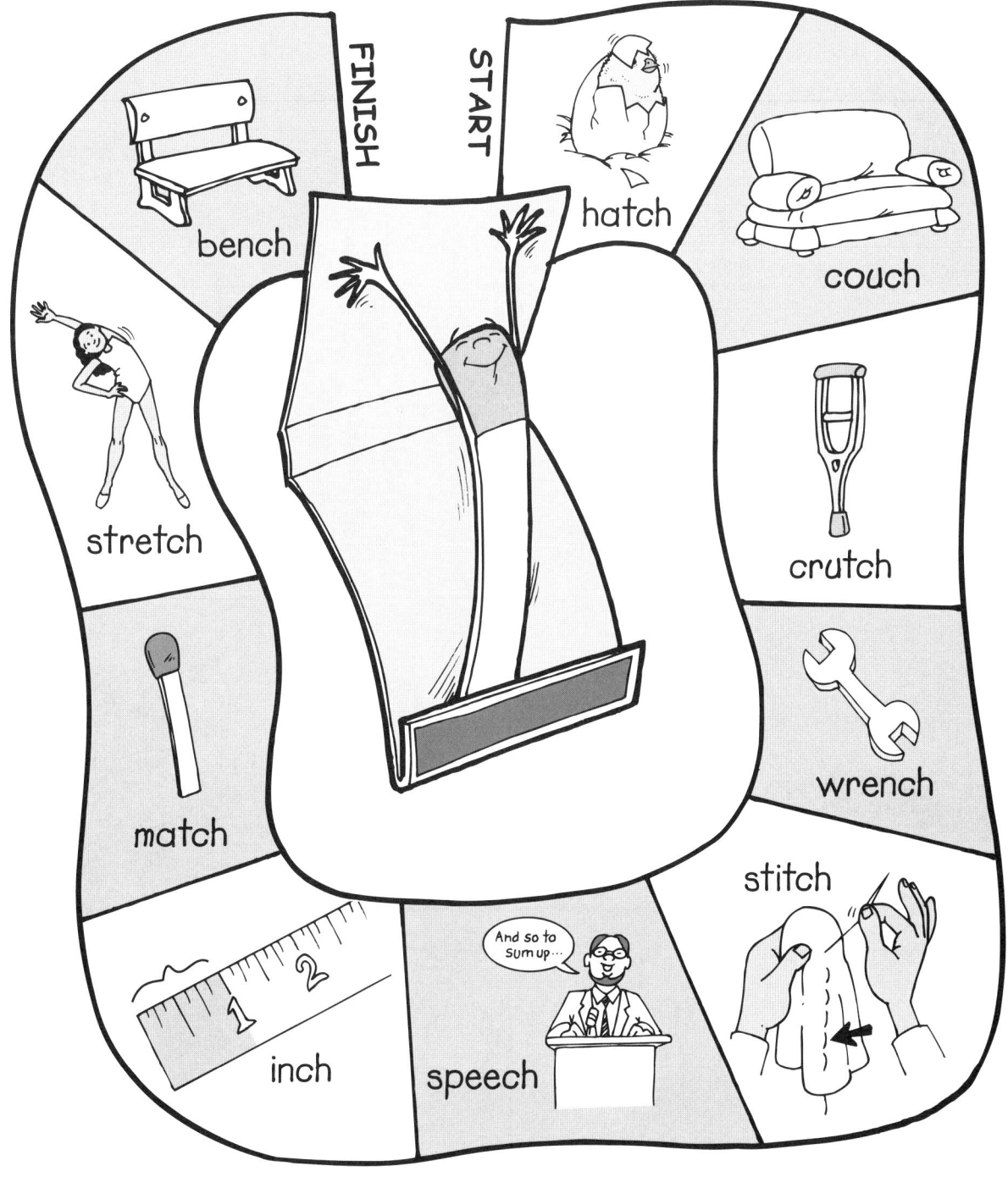

Final
Spotlight on Articulation – CH

CH and SH Pairs

Name _____

Look at the pictures in each box. Listen as someone says the name of each picture. Decide which one ends with the CH sound and circle it. Then name that picture using a good CH sound.

Answers: 1. watch 2. witch 3. brunch 4. crutch 5. latch 6. catch 7. hutch 8. match

CH Tic-Tac-Toe

Name _____

Listen as someone says each word that ends with the CH sound. Find the word and say it. Then circle the letters that make the CH sound at the end of the word. When you're finished, play tic-tac-toe!

torch	march	branch
coach	porch	touch
reach	patch	watch

brunch	itch	crunch
switch	each	which
sketch	ouch	speech

match	batch	touch
ranch	punch	beach
wrench	reach	hutch

grouch	ostrich	punch
latch	catch	ditch
roach	attach	French

Final
Spotlight on Articulation – CH

Wrestling Match

Name _____

Read this story aloud. Don't forget to use a good CH sound.

It was time for the [wrestling match]. The wrestlers sat on the [bench]. The [coach] handed each one a [peach]. Then he gave a [speech].

The [coach] had all of the wrestlers [stretch]. It was important to [stretch] so no one would get hurt.

When the [wrestling match] was over, the [coach] was very happy. The team won! The [coach] took everyone out for [lunch] to celebrate.

Final
Spotlight on Articulation – CH

Back Porch

Name _____

Find all the pictures of words that end with the CH sound. Then tell about the picture using a good CH sound.

Key words: arch, bench, branch, fetch, hopscotch, itch, Mitch, perch, porch, scratch, switch

Final
Spotlight on Articulation – CH

Mr. Hatch and Patch

Name _____

Listen to the story. Then cut the pictures apart. Put the pictures in order and retell the story. Don't forget to use a good CH sound.

Mr. Hatch was trying to teach his dog, Patch, to fetch.

Mr. Hatch threw a branch and said, "Watch it, Patch! Go get it!"

Patch ran to get the branch. He brought it back and put it on the bench.

Mr. Hatch said, "Good boy, Patch!" Mr. Hatch and Patch played fetch all afternoon.

CH Fill-In Sentences

Name _____

Say the words in the box. Fill in each sentence with a word from the box. Then say each sentence using a good CH sound.

Arch	bleach	hatch	speech
attach	butterscotch	scratch	stagecoach
avalanche	each	sketch	stopwatch

1. An _____ can be very dangerous.

2. The coach started the _____ at the beginning of the race.

3. You need _____ to get white clothes clean.

4. The eggs in the nest were about to _____.

5. In St. Louis, it is interesting to visit the _____.

6. You'll need a big nail to _____ the rope to the house.

7. Danny goes to _____ class three times a week.

8. Rich got a long _____ on his arm from his cat.

9. The artist drew a quick _____ of the baby.

10. Some pioneers traveled by _____.

11. I love to put _____ topping on my ice cream.

12. Please give _____ student a sheet of paper.

Answers: avalanche, stopwatch, bleach, hatch, Arch, attach, speech, scratch, sketch, stagecoach, butterscotch, each

Final
Spotlight on Articulation – CH

CH Monster

Name _____

Draw a line from the CH to pictures of words with the CH sound in the middle. Then name those pictures using a good CH sound.

Answers: branches, hatchet, orchard, peaches, teacher, watches

Medial
Spotlight on Articulation – CH

What's Your Fortune?

Name _____

Cross out the pictures of words that don't have the CH sound in the middle. Then name the other pictures using a good CH sound.

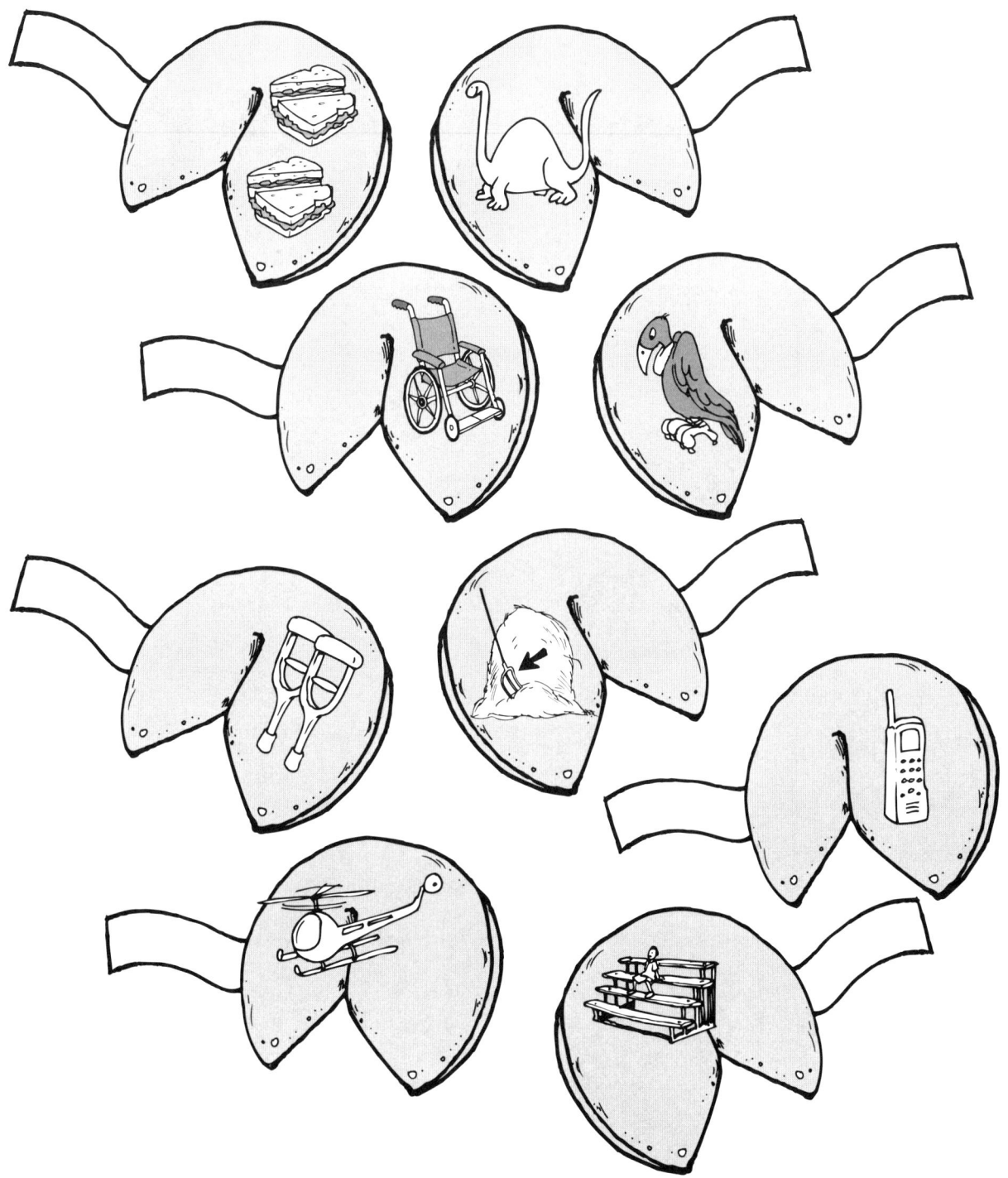

Cross Out: dinosaur, helicopter, telephone
Name: bleachers, crutches, pitchfork, sandwiches, vulture, wheelchair

Medial
Spotlight on Articulation – CH

CH, CH, CH!

Name _____

Toss a penny. Heads—move one space. Tails—move two spaces. Name each picture along the way using a good CH sound.

Medial
Spotlight on Articulation – CH

CH Tic-Tac-Toe

Name _____

Listen as someone says each word. Find the word and say it. Then circle the letters that make the CH sound in the middle of the word. When you're finished, play tic-tac-toe!

crunchy	poncho	patches
teacher	kitchen	benches
pitcher	nacho	ketchup

roaches	peachy	pitchfork
hatchet	vulture	sketching
lunches	statue	watching

branches	future	stitches
catcher	nature	touching
reaching	inches	matches

achieve	natural	hatching
bunches	ditches	crouching
switches	itchy	grandchild

Medial
Spotlight on Articulation – CH

CH-ing!

Name _____

Say each verb. Then add *-ing* to the verb. Write or say the new word using a good CH sound. Then use it in a sentence.

watch _____

pitch _____

catch _____

match _____

march _____

reach _____

sketch _____

stretch _____

teach _____

touch _____

Answers: watching, pitching, catching, matching, marching, reaching, sketching, stretching, teaching, touching

At the Zoo

Name _____

Read this story aloud. Don't forget to use a good CH sound.

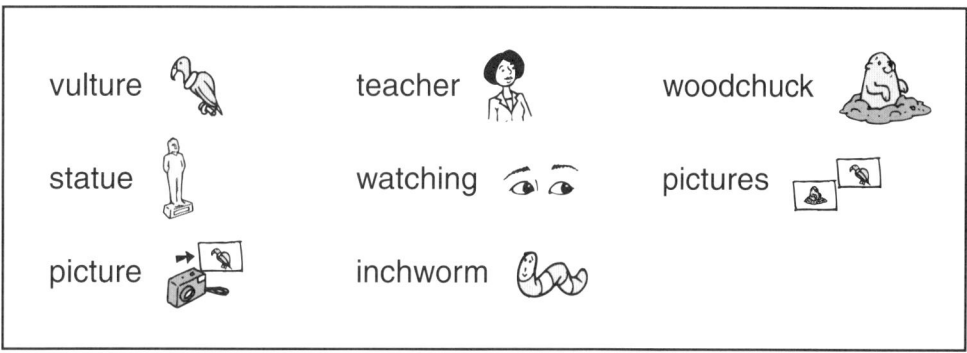

We went to the zoo. The first animal we saw was a 🦅 (vulture). It was on a 🗿 (statue). I took a 📷 (picture) of the 🦅 (vulture) for my 👩 (teacher). While I was 👀 (watching), the 🦅 (vulture) ate an 🐛 (inchworm).

The next animal we saw was a 🦫 (woodchuck). I knew that my 👩 (teacher) would like a 📷 (picture) of the 🦫 (woodchuck) too.

I had fun taking 📷 (pictures) of the animals at the zoo.

A Day at the Park

Name _____

Find all the pictures of words that have a CH sound in the middle. Then tell about the picture using a good CH sound.

Key words: benches, hatching, ketchup, nachos, orchard, peaches, pitcher, poncho, sandwiches, watching

Not So Lucky Key Chain

Name _____

Listen to the story. Then cut the pictures apart. Put the pictures in order and retell the story. Don't forget to use a good CH sound.

Rachel got up from the bleachers.
She was the catcher for the Woodchucks.

Rachel held onto her lucky key chain as she jumped over one of the benches.

The pitcher pitched the first ball.
It hit Rachel right on her knee.

Rachel didn't need stitches, but she needed to use crutches for a while.
I guess that key chain wasn't so lucky!

CH Fill-In Sentences

Name _____

Say the words in the box. Fill in each sentence with a word from the box. Then say each sentence using a good CH sound.

anchovies	butcher	matches	signature
Archery	handkerchief	nachos	stitches
branches	inches	nature	temperature

1. The _____ dropped 20 degrees in an hour.

2. Richie likes _____ on his pizza.

3. Adam had to get three _____ in his knee.

4. Please write your _____ on the bottom line of the contract.

5. He had a big plate of _____ for lunch.

6. The oak tree's _____ swayed in the wind.

7. _____ is my favorite activity at Boy Scout camp.

8. The _____ cut the meat into several pieces.

9. You can't start a fire with wet _____.

10. Derek grew five _____ over the summer.

11. Use a tissue or a _____ when you blow your nose.

12. Flowers are a beautiful part of _____.

Answers: temperature, anchovies, stitches, signature, nachos, branches, Archery, butcher, matches, inches, handkerchief, nature

Medial
Spotlight on Articulation – CH

CH Rows

Name _____

Look at the first picture in each row. Does it have the CH sound at the beginning, at the end, or in the middle of the word? Circle the pictures of words in that row that have the CH sound in the same place.

1.
2.
3.
4.
5.

Answers: 1. lunch, bench, watch; 2. chick: cheetah, cherry; 3. kitchen: vulture, pitcher; 4. ostrich: perch, sandwich; 5. chicken: chocolate, chain

Initial, Final, and Medial
Spotlight on Articulation – CH

Richie Helps His Dad

Name _____

Read this story aloud. Don't forget to use a good CH sound.

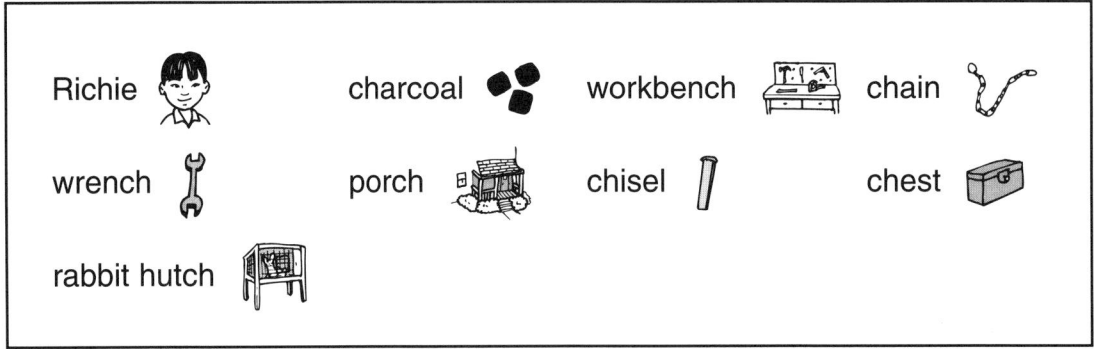

Yesterday, [Richie] helped his dad. First he got a [wrench] and tightened the bolts on the [rabbit hutch]. Next [Richie] cleaned up the [charcoal] that had spilled. He put the bag of [charcoal] next to the [porch].

Then [Richie] helped his dad clean up the [workbench]. He hung the [chisel] next to the [wrench]. Then he rolled up a [chain] and put it in the [chest].

[Richie]'s dad said, "You're a good helper, [Richie]. Thank you!"

Initial, Final, and Medial
Spotlight on Articulation – CH

Go, Team, Go!

Name _____

Find all the pictures of words that have a CH sound. Then tell about the picture using a good CH sound.

Key words: bench, bleachers, chain, chasing, cheering, cheerleaders, Chihuahua, chipmunk, coach, crutches, touchdown, watching

Inchy's Adventure

Name _____

Listen to the story. Then cut the pictures apart. Put the pictures in order and retell the story. Don't forget to use a good CH sound.

Inchy the Inchworm was on an adventure. He wanted to see what the kitchen looked like. He cheerfully began to crawl across the kitchen floor.

It was an interesting adventure for Inchy. He had to climb over two checkers and go around a lunch box.

When he was hungry, he found a piece of cheese on the floor. He chewed it all up.

Inchy slowly made his way across the floor, inch by inch. When he got across the kitchen, he cheered. What a great adventure for Inchy!

Initial, Final, and Medial
Spotlight on Articulation – CH

CH Fill-In Sentences

Name _____

Say the words in the box. Fill in each sentence with a word from the box. Then say each sentence using a good CH sound.

challenging	chuckled	hatchet	poach
Chestnuts	cross-stitch	mix and match	pork chops
choose	French fries	pitchfork	unlatch

1. We are going to cook _____ on the grill.

2. Kelly ordered a hamburger and _____.

3. The farmer spread the hay with the _____.

4. My uncle chopped up the wood with a _____.

5. _____ are round nuts that grow on trees.

6. Evan had to _____ which color to use.

7. The obstacle course was really _____.

8. Jake _____ when he heard the joke.

9. You can _____ the pieces to make lots of different designs.

10. Please _____ the gate so I can come in.

11. My aunt taught me how to _____.

12. I want to learn how to _____ an egg.

Answers: pork chops, French fries, pitchfork, hatchet, Chestnuts, choose, challenging, chuckled, mix and match, unlatch, cross-stitch, poach

Progress Chart

_____ Name   _____ School

_____ Grade   _____ Speech-Language Pathologist

Date	Target Sound	Level (Syllable, Word, Sentence)	Word Position (I, M, F)	# Correct/Total	% Correct

Comments: _____

_____